THE
# HARD
*Questions*
for Adult Children and
Their Aging Parents

Also by Susan Piver

*The Hard Questions: 100 Essential Questions to Ask Before You Say "I Do"*

*The Hard Questions for an Authentic Life: 100 Essential Questions
for Designing Your Life from the Inside Out*

100 ESSENTIAL QUESTIONS
FOR FACING THE FUTURE TOGETHER,
WITH COURAGE AND COMPASSION

# THE HARD *Questions*

## for Adult Children and Their Aging Parents

# Susan Piver

GOTHAM BOOKS

GOTHAM BOOKS
Published by Penguin Group (USA) Inc.
375 Hudson Street, New York, New York 10014, U.S.A.
Penguin Group (Canada) 10 Alcorn Avenue, Toronto, Ontario, Canada M4V 3B2
(a division of Pearson Penguin Canada Inc.)
Penguin Books Ltd, 80 Strand, London WC2R 0RL, England
Penguin Ireland, 25 St Stephen's Green, Dublin 2, Ireland (a division of Penguin Books Ltd)
Penguin Group (Australia), 250 Camberwell Road, Camberwell, Victoria 3124, Australia
(a division of Pearson Australia Group Pty Ltd)
Penguin Books India Pvt Ltd, 11 Community Centre, Panchsheel Park, New Delhi - 110 017, India
Penguin Group (NZ), Cnr Airborne and Rosedale Roads, Albany, Auckland, New Zealand
(a division of Pearson New Zealand Ltd)
Penguin Books (South Africa) (Pty) Ltd, 24 Sturdee Avenue,
Rosebank, Johannesburg 2196, South Africa

Penguin Books Ltd, Registered Offices: 80 Strand, London WC2R 0RL, England

Published by Gotham Books, a division of Penguin Group (USA) Inc.

First printing, October 2004
1   3   5   7   9   10   8   6   4   2

LIBRARY OF CONGRESS CATALOGING-IN-PUBLICATION DATA

Piver, Susan, 1957–
    The hard questions for adult children and their aging parents : 100 essential questions for facing
the future together with courage and compassion / Susan Piver.
    p.  cm.
    ISBN 1-592-40077-9 (hardcover : alk. paper)
    1. Aging parents. 2. Adult children of aging parents. I. Title.
    HQ1063.6.P59 2004
    306.874—dc22                                                                2004012539

Printed in the United States of America
Set in Weiss
Designed by Jaye Zimet

*For David Piver and Carol Piver Hanna, in gratitude for our deep connection
as siblings and friends.*

*For our beloved mother and father, Louise and Julius Piver, with love that has no end.*

# CONTENTS

# ACKNOWLEDGMENTS

With appreciation for their willingness to share their stories, hearts, ideas, and support, a deep bow to Helen Abel, Josh Baran, Richard Borofsky, Michael Carroll, Amy Elizabeth Fox, Beth Grossman, Judith Kern, Joseph Kociubes, Susanna Lack, Judith Lief, Linda Loewenthal, Joel H. Marcus, Bill McKeever, Justin Morreale, Belleruth Naparstek, Richard Pine, Judith Putman-Sette, Patricia Reinstein, Jill Satterfield, Barry Sternfeld, Cornelia Tenney, Eliot Vestner, Jeff Waltcher, Laura Yanne.

And, as always, thanks to Duncan Browne for his steadiness, encouragement, and love.

# INTRODUCTION

When I was about ten years old, my mother began telling me what a good daughter I had been to her and saying that when she died (which, she always made sure to add, would not happen for a very, *very* long time), I should harbor no regrets about our relationship.

She has reiterated those words periodically over the last thirty-plus years. She has said them during periods when we got along, when we fought, when I was a child, and into my own middle age. She has said them when she really meant them and when it would have been almost impossible to mean them.

My mother's own mother died at just about the time she began offering her reassurances to me. And, as she lay in her hospital room with her four daughters gathered about her, my grandmother had said those very same words to them—that she loved them, that they had been wonderful daughters to her, and that they should have no regrets after she passed.

I know that my grandmother's words brought enormous comfort

to my mother in the years that followed. She hasn't wondered if she should have done or said anything differently during her mother's life. And while I'm sure she has wished many times that her mother could have known her grandchildren better, attended this or that family event, been available to talk on the phone about life's big and small events, she has never, to my knowledge, regretted any aspect of their relationship.

While I didn't make the connection at the time, I now realize that my mother wanted to bestow the gift her mother had given her on me and my siblings as soon as possible. When I was small she only mentioned it now and then, and I barely listened to what she was saying, except to tune in very carefully to the part that went, "it will not happen for a very, *very* long time." Sometimes, depending on the amount of terror she saw on my face, she would add several more "verys."

As a teenager, I vacillated between moments of painful, gasping terror that she might actually die and a sort of spiteful hope that she would, both of which emotions were immediately followed by numerous superstitious gestures and phrases to counter the effect of my thoughts on her lifespan. I still didn't think she or my dad would ever really die, though.

When I was in my twenties, their deaths continued to seem quite impossible, but I began to admit to myself for several seconds at a time that my parents were actually mortal. Then, in my thirties, I began to take the idea seriously. My younger sister and I admitted to each other that we thought about our parents' death, but all we could do was cry and promise to be there for each other through this unthinkable eventuality.

My mother continues every now and then to tell me that I am a good daughter and should have no regrets. But now she's in her seventies, I'm in my forties, and I'm hearing her in a very different way. Suddenly, on some level, it's as if I'm taking these words in for the first time and allowing myself to contemplate them. Have I really been a good daughter? Are there things I'll regret? Are there things she regrets? What will it be like to lose each other? What details and plans do we need to think through? What does she really expect and want from me as she ages and reconciles with life's end?

I believe (and hope) that all families can benefit from having such conversations *on their own terms and about the issues that are specifically important to them*, and so there are no answers in this book—only questions. Each of us will have our own way of engaging our minds, and the minds of our family, in this conversation. Comfort levels will vary from family to family, and from topic to topic within each family. That's as it should be. For some, this dialogue will be an act of love and affection. For others, it will be about taking care of business and tying up loose ends. Or it may be both. There is clearly no right or wrong here. I encourage each family to review the questions and choose only those that are most appropriate—or useful—for them at this time.

How can we find the courage to contemplate the death of our parents? How can we best accompany them as they age? No matter how close or distant the relationship, it seems almost impossible—not to mention undesirable, upsetting, disorienting, and so much more—to imagine life without them. Why would anyone *want* to spend time thinking about such a thing? Or, even more unthinkable, talking about it together?

Some answers to these questions emerge when we begin considering what is likely to happen if we don't think or talk with our parents about their aging and death. There are consequences ranging from the practical (do they have life insurance?) to the emotional (is there anything we might later regret not having talked about?) to the spiritual (what prayers or rituals would they like me to observe on their behalf, in the moments or days following their death?). Ignoring these issues out of fear, denial, or procrastination can set us up to "miss" (or misinterpret) both our own and our parents' needs, hopes, fears, and longings as we contemplate and they themselves reconcile with their life's end.

Beyond these reasons—the practical, emotional, and spiritual—

there is another consideration in thinking about our parents' life and death, and talking with them about it all. Whether our relationship is emotionally healthy or unhealthy, nourishing or unwholesome, reciprocated or unrequited, asking these questions is every child's opportunity to in some way honor his or her parents for the gift of life given. If the relationship has been close (and there is usually at least some feeling of warmth, even in unhappy relationships), it is an opportunity to concentrate one's gratitude into the essential gifts of time, attention, and loving-kindness. If the relationship has been more painful than not, if one harbors feelings of fear or anger (and even in the healthiest families, there is always some of this), it is an opportunity to transcend the relationship to which you've grown accustomed, and, if only briefly, to establish one that is sane, gentle, and appropriate for this time in both your lives.

As mentioned, the questions in this book cover a variety of topics. There are questions about finances, legalities, and housing. There are questions about religious beliefs, relationship issues, and legacy. But, in asking these questions with my own parents, I have found it impossible to separate the practical from the spiritual or emotional because, invariably, when you consider a question such as "Who would make decisions for you if you were not capable of making them for yourself?" both practical considerations *and* spiritual values and beliefs rise to the surface.

Practical considerations might include assigning responsibility for executing the appropriate paperwork and/or contacting experts or advisors who can help you implement whatever decision your parents make. But at the same time, no matter what those decisions might be, other important questions arise: questions of affection (who do your parents feel close to) and of values (who do they really trust). Even questions that seem purely pragmatic ("Where are your important papers kept?") can arouse very deep feelings. They may evoke issues of trust, failure, and loss of control—or none of these. Perhaps your parents are ambivalent or worried about disclosing the contents of one document or another, and telling you where those documents are kept would open the door to those feelings. It's important to be aware of the emotions that might accompany even the most straightforward questions.

Similarly, so-called spiritual questions such as "What are your beliefs about the afterlife?" can actually have practical implications in terms of burial rituals, choosing a funeral officiant, and so on. So don't be surprised if seemingly simple questions result in profound discussion, or if deeply sacred questions lead to conversations about finances, logistics, or other such mundane topics. In fact, this idea that the practical and the spiritual are not separate will never be more self-evident than when you and your parents are relating to end-of-life issues together.

## How to Answer The Hard Questions

### Intention

Before you begin to ask the questions in this book, please take some time to examine your own intentions in wanting to do so. You may be motivated by a wish to "take care of business" for yourself and/or your parents. You may have an intuition that it's simply time to have this conversation. You may have just learned that a parent is seriously ill and need advice about what issues require your consideration. You may be anticipating conflict or confusion with parents or siblings and want to take precautions to avoid such. You may be worried about the impact your parents' medical and/or financial situations may eventually have on you and your family. You may be feeling that you and your parents are somehow in need of one another's support although neither of you knows quite how to ask for or offer it. There are many other possibilities, and it's likely that, for each reader, there will be a mix of intentions. Examining those intentions is critical to ensuring that the process is as helpful as possible. They will lead you to the questions that are most appropriate for you.

And no matter what the course or present state of your relationship with your parents, finding a way to speak and act from love or respect (however you define it) can ensure that this dialogue has lasting benefit for all involved. So please examine your heart. Try to find the place from which you can lead with your parents' benefit in mind, no matter what other feelings may also be present as you enter this dialogue.

*Self-Inquiry*

The next step is for each participant to review The Hard Questions on his or her own. Decide which questions seem really useful and which seem less so (realizing that siblings or parents may feel otherwise). Make note of which ones you're especially eager to have answered, which seem important, irrelevant, easy, or difficult. Without second-guessing their responses, try to imagine which questions are likely to be inspiring or frightening to your siblings or parents.

If you have a spouse or partner, it may also be useful to let him or her know you're planning on having a Hard Questions conversation with your parents, and to review some of the questions together. Some answers may have serious impact on your own family. For example, when you ask your parents, "If one or both of you need and/or desire managed care, could you afford to pay for it?" should the answer be "No, we need you to help us out financially," it would be good to know your partner's feelings about such a possibility. Similarly, questions about finances, health care, and legalities can have consequences for your personal life and, therefore, your partner's.

*Dialogue with Siblings*

Once you've taken stock of your intentions, thoughts, and feelings, the next step is to check in with your siblings. Although this process can certainly be undertaken by one sibling alone, it may be important to discuss with your brothers and sisters the risks and rewards in answering The Hard Questions as a family. Some siblings might be upset if you undertook this dialogue without consulting them first. In other families, one child might live near their parents while the others are far away—leaving the bulk of emotional, fiscal, and logistical responsibilities to that one sibling. Or, one sibling might be close to his or her parents while the others are estranged. But whatever the interpersonal dynamics or geographic realities, I can almost guarantee that every family member will have an emotional and spiritual stake in the outcome. It would, therefore, be best to at least acknowledge this reality at the outset, however the actual dialogue with your parents proceeds.

While there are, no doubt, exceptions to this rule, I have found, in discussing this book with friends, family, and experts, that, in most families, there is an unstated understanding that one sibling has or will have the primary responsibility for relating to his or her parents as they age. We usually know who that sibling is, whether we discuss it or not. In my husband's family, for example, he was the sibling most intimately involved in caring for his mother. He made practical, day-to-day decisions, kept the rest of the family current, and collected their input in order to make financial and legal decisions. He was "the one." In my family, I know I'm not "the one"; my sister is. In our particular families these roles evolved naturally and truly feel right. For others, however, it can be useful to explore expectations about who feels responsible for what as parents age— and especially to focus on each sibling's comfort level with the way responsibilities are allocated or assumed.

Special (and perhaps especially difficult) issues will come to light if either or both of your parents have been divorced (and possibly remarried). If you have stepparents or stepsiblings, each family will need to decide if it's possible or desirable to speak to divorced parents together, individually, or with his or her current spouse, should there be one. Similarly, if you have stepsiblings, give some thought to what it will mean to include or exclude them. Which is most appropriate? If your stepsiblings and you have been a family since you were small, it may be unthinkable to have conversations without them. If, on the other hand, your stepsiblings came into your life after you all reached adulthood, there may be no natural or sensible reason to pursue this dialogue as a group. Think carefully about your particular family dynamic; the potential emotional, financial, and/or legal ramifications; and make the best decision you can.

*Timing and Choosing Relevant Questions*

Before embarking on this process, make note of your parents' current state of health and well-being. There are three broad possibilities, each of which will have particular implications for how you proceed and which questions will be most important. They may be healthy and basically living the same life they've always lived. They may be in the early stages of illness or beginning to notice that physical and/or mental frailties require a shift in their accustomed lifestyle. Or, they may already be acutely ill or dying. There will be questions that are appropriate or inappropriate for each of these situations. Feel free to pick and choose among them. But please remember that whether your parents are healthy and vital, diminished and withdrawn, healthy and in managed care, or ill and in a nursing home or hospice, the process can still be beneficial.

That said, I believe it would be most helpful to ask them sooner rather than later, when your parents are most capable of participating effectively in the conversation, although their answers may well change as or if illness occurs, if or when one of them dies, or should family dynamics shift. These questions aren't meant to evoke sworn testimony, but to give a sense of how everyone is thinking and feeling at the time they are asked.

*Explore with Parents*

Are your parents open to asking and answering The Hard Questions with you and your siblings? There is only one way to find out: Ask them. There's a variety of ways to broach the subject, ranging from the direct ("Mom, Dad, I'd like to talk about your health, finances, and our relationship. As we all get older, I'm realizing more and more how important it is to discuss these things") to the emotional ("I love you and want to know everything there is to know so I can be as supportive and loving as possible at this time in your life") to the pragmatic ("How would you feel about going over a couple of issues about your finances?"). Remember, you don't have to ask *all* The Hard Questions at one sitting, or ever. You can start with a few, see how that goes, and then decide whether to keep going. You can even use this book as an "excuse" to initiate the dialogue ("Hey, I was skimming over this interesting book on adult children and their parents. Some of the points seem useful; would it be okay if we looked at them together?").

Of course, it's easy to see why it's important for parents and children to discuss these topics; what's not so easy is to actually do it. No matter how practical and prepared or how committed you are to acting responsibly and lovingly toward yourself, your siblings, and your parents, it's still difficult to actually have this conversation.

Most of us are afraid to even try. Some families have financial complexities or deficiencies that can make conversation difficult. Some may be experiencing serious health-related problems. Others have long-standing emotional issues that can add to the stress of this dialogue. It's also possible that someone in the family—a sibling or a parent—will not want to do this at all. One or both parents may be feeling enough anxiety, depression, or denial to prevent them from even considering this dialogue. This is a completely understandable but difficult obstacle to overcome. Should you encounter this situation, try to find some small question or topic you *can* address together. Then, if it goes well, you may be able to introduce a second, fairly nonthreatening question, and so on until you get as far as you are able.

No matter what your particular situation, there are four qualities that can help you navigate The Hard Questions with the skillfulness that is necessary for a meaningful outcome.

*Courage*

As I've already said, you need courage to even contemplate the death of your parents. Courage is the willingness to step into whatever may be arising within yourself and in your world, no matter what it is. It is the intention to go beyond fear, beyond your comfort level, for your own benefit and the benefit of others.

When we think about our parents' death, our first reaction, usually, is fear—of their suffering, of our own pain in the face of their suffering, of what it will be like when death actually occurs. Whether it manifests as sadness, frustration, obsessive detail management, or simply denial, fear generally lurks just below the surface. It's extremely important to step into *and* beyond this fear in order to be of service to our parents when they need us. We must be brave enough to step beyond our own comfort level to what will be most helpful to them and to us.

*The Willingness to Feel*

When you open yourself to the realities of death and dying within your own family, deep and compelling emotions may arise. At first, these feelings can be extremely, even unbearably uncomfortable, tempting you to do whatever you can to stop feeling the sadness, anger, anxiety, or whatever emotion may arise. I'm not saying you should *force* yourself to feel bad, but if and when these feelings do arise, allowing yourself to feel them can be powerful, beneficial, and, ultimately, can deepen your ability to tolerate whatever may arise. When you are sad, cry. When you become angry or irritated, yell and scream, go to the gym, or vent your feelings with a friend or counselor. When you become anxious, let the anxiety shake through you. Don't try to distract yourself by talking yourself out of it, sentimentalizing it, throwing yourself into work to avoid it, rationalizing it, fighting it, blaming others for it, or trying to ignore it. Simply feel what you are feeling without having to provide it with a "story line." If, for example, you feel sadness as you contemplate a parent's passing, you can feel the sadness without telling yourself that if only you had been a better daughter (or son), you wouldn't feel so sad, or that this sadness means you have to immediately become a hospice volunteer, or that when your parents die you'll feel so alone on your birthday, or anything else. These "story lines" may, indeed, be quite true, but they actually prevent the proper "metabolization" of feeling. They prolong, misconstrue, or complicate the feeling beyond its original form. When you are able to simply feel your feelings, you don't become stuck in any one of them or frozen in fear of another. And at no time will this ability be more useful—to you and to those around you—than when you are working with the aging and death of your parents. The willingness to feel is what will enable you to stay emotionally connected to them when all you want to do is withdraw, and to yourself as you begin to contemplate your own aging and death.

*The Willingness to Relinquish Control*

If you cultivate courage and an ability to tolerate your own and others' strong emotions, you will have established a strong position from which to contemplate and accept perhaps the most difficult truth of all—your inability to control outcomes. We all crave certainty. We're taught to believe that if we are prepared, conscientious, kindhearted, and intelligent, we can actually direct the events of our lives. We each have our own strategies and mantras for securing and ensuring our own happiness. We have formulas for finding a mate (Get out and socialize! Lose five pounds! Visualize him or her!), getting the perfect job (Dream big! Be aggressive! Believe!), or even raising healthy children (No TV! Religious training! Family outings!), and so on. But while all these admonitions may be helpful, none of them can guarantee the certainty we crave. Yet, time after time, in our own families, at school, at work, and in intimate relationships, we try to set up situations we can count on to make us happy. And at no time is this wish for certainty stronger than when we think about losing a loved one. Whether it's our spouse (whom we've already asked to promise never to leave us), our child (to whom we issue a continuous stream of instructions for remaining safe and happy), or our parents, we can't actually have power over the outcomes of our relationships. Although this is a very painful truth to live with, addressing the questions of aging and death is a sure way to begin accepting these realities. At first, our acceptance may be only theoretical, which is okay. Anything we can do to acclimate to this reality is good. But when a parent becomes ill or dies, there is no more theory, only the pain or shock of loss, and the recognition that, no matter what, we can't alter or prevent what is happening. Maintaining an open heart, continuing to offer and receive love, *staying present* with yourself, your siblings, and your parents, without becoming too enmeshed in "managing" the situation *or* drowning in your own emotions, is actually the most helpful gesture you can make.

*Presence*

How is it possible to stay present in the face of such powerful and painful feelings? What does "staying present" mean, anyway? One definition of staying present is trying to do the first three steps—have courage, be open to feeling, and be willing to relinquish control—all the time. If you have courage, are willing to feel, and relinquish the idea that you can control outcomes, you will have gone a long way toward cultivating presence. When you are present, you open yourself to what *is* with curiosity, gentleness, and accuracy—which enables you to *be with* whatever is arising in a wholehearted way. And what your parents most likely want from you, more than anything, is for you simply to be with them until the end of their lives. Ultimately, this is the only—and best—gift you can give.

*    *    *

While, as I've said, it's not important for you to answer every single question in this book, it will be useful to consider and answer as many as seem relevant to you. Each family will certainly have emotional, psychological, and practical issues that make some questions seem crucial while others are totally off-limits. So please use your best judgment when choosing the questions you think are most valuable.

That said, however, reviewing all the questions will give you a clear sense of how to accompany, honor, and support your parents as they navigate toward the end of their lives. And answering as many of them as seems pertinent will help you to prepare—emotionally, psychologically, spiritually, and pragmatically—to deal with what is bound to be a scary, painful, even kind of crazy time. To do that is like taking a preliminary tour of a journey you unknowingly "signed up for" some forty or fifty years ago. The more you can anticipate the climate, terrain, and customs of the place you may be visiting, the more likely it is that you will navigate with skill and care. In addition, as your parents age and after their deaths, many details of their world may fall to you for resolution. The more you know about that world in advance, the more likely it is that you, your siblings, and anyone else who is involved will be able to manage the situation peacefully together.

\* \* \*

The questions in this book are meant to support your family in coming to terms with a parent's aging and death. They offer a way to start thinking through a host of involved and potentially painful issues but are not meant to provide comprehensive solutions to all the complex issues you will face together. Depending on your intentions, your sibling relationships, your relationship with your parents, and their current state of health, these questions can be used to create a simple, straightforward checklist of key issues, or they can be used as a means to connect with one another emotionally and spiritually. Please feel free to use them in the way that is right for you.

Note: The process of asking The Hard Questions can be initiated by either children or parents. Except for those in the first two chapters, however, for reasons of linguistic clarity and simplicity, I've written them from the point of view of the children. Parents should, nevertheless, feel free to reverse the pronouns and approach them from their own perspective.

# THE
# HARD
## Questions
### for Adult Children and
### Their Aging Parents

## ✦ CHAPTER 1 ✦
# For Self and Siblings Only

I would suggest that before you begin to ask and answer any of The Hard Questions with your parents, you should, if at all possible, discuss the possibility of doing so with your siblings. It's been shown time and again that even though you theoretically grew up in the same environment, raised by the same parents, your experiences, feelings about, or perceptions of those experiences may be different. And your current financial, psychological, and spiritual situations may also be different. Any or all of those differences may affect the way you view the possibility of broaching various subjects with your parents, and so, if you have a close—or at least non-contentious—relationship with your brothers and sisters, it may be healthiest to pursue this conversation among yourselves before approaching your parents.

Remember, the answers to questions about finances and legalities can have a very real impact on every one of you. If, for example, after your parents have passed away, the family home is to be sold, each sibling may have his or her own opinion about how it would be best—both financially and emotionally—to carry out that responsibility.

And, questions relating to relationships and spirituality—even more than those relating to finances or other purely practical matters—can have profound emotional effects, for good or for ill, on each sibling in a very different way.

It might be useful, therefore, to begin the conversation with your siblings by asking each of them to share his or her particular insights and feelings about which issues to address and which to leave alone, so that you can try to come to consensus about which questions it will be most important for you to discuss with your parents.

If you can't agree to discuss every area suggested in this book, try to come up with one (finances, health care, or spirituality, for example) that you *all* feel comfortable pursuing—with the agreement that, if the conversation goes well, you will try to pursue a second area, and then perhaps a third.

Or, if you can't agree on one entire set of questions to pursue, try to come up with just two or three, taken from one subject area or several. Then, if that goes well, perhaps you'll agree to ask more. It's totally fine to take this process one small step at a time.

It's tempting to do one of two things with our aging parents: figure "this is the last chance, I better express all my pent-up feelings now," or "forget about it; it's too late to make any difference anyway." Anger and sadness are likely to be the emotions underlying both these impulses. If you or your siblings are experiencing either one, it's important to ask yourselves—and one another—whether it's possible to set those feelings aside in order to serve your parents' needs, as well as your own, by trying to learn more about *their* hopes and fears at this time in their life. Can you express your feelings in a way that is appropriate and skillful? Is your intention in wanting to do so based in love more than fear? Can your siblings also do this? The greater the certainty with which you and your siblings are able to answer these questions, the better you will be able to judge the best time, atmosphere, and rhythm for approaching The Hard Questions with your parents.

Needless to say, sorting through each sibling's emotional, spiritual, and practical "agenda" can be complicated at best. Depending upon the dynamics that govern your relationship, any one of the following outcomes may result:

- You choose to bypass your siblings entirely because you believe they won't have any interest in the outcome or will disrupt the process completely, and you go to your parents directly.

- You inform your siblings that you're going to have this conversation with your parents and just want them to be aware that you're doing so.
- You alone have the dialogue with your parents, but you report the outcome to siblings.
- You and your siblings select a subset of important questions (that is, only those about finances, or only those relating to spiritual beliefs) and pursue a family dialogue about that specific topic.
- You and your siblings decide that one of you will discuss The Hard Questions (all or a subset) with your parents on everyone's behalf.
- You plan and carry out the dialogue together.

There is no one choice that is correct for everyone, but if there's any way to promote healing, openness, and a deeper emotional connection among you, your siblings, and your parents, it would be brave to choose the option that provides the greatest likelihood of that outcome.

And, of course, if it's deemed wise, it can be useful to bring in a therapist, advisor, mediator, family friend, or pastoral counselor should you and your siblings need one in order to caringly and effectively relate with each other and your parents. These are vitally important questions with potentially serious consequences, both practically and spiritually. I encourage you to take the process very seriously and not hesitate to do whatever you feel is needed to bring healing, meaning, and authenticity to the exchange.

Even if you're an only child, it can be helpful to review the questions on your own before bringing them up with your parents. Or, if you prefer, ask a trusted friend to help you think them through. Preparing in advance, whether you are one of a large family or have no siblings at all, can help to ensure a more loving and practical conversation.

1. What is making me/us want to enter into this dialogue at this time with my/our parents? List two or three (or more) specific outcomes I/we hope to achieve (for example, a housing plan should one or both parents become incapacitated; a list of important contacts such as doctors, lawyers, and so forth; a robust discussion about family history and lineage; clarity about how our parents' assets might be distributed).

_____

_____

_____

_____

_____

_____

_____

_____

2. What emotional and/or practical outcomes do we hope for?
   Which do we fear?

_____

_____

_____

_____

_____

_____

_____

3. Will our parents welcome this discussion? One? Both? Neither?

_____

_____

_____

_____

_____

_____

_____

4. Should we siblings all talk to both our parents together?
   Would it be better to speak to each of them separately? Should

one sibling be designated as spokesperson for all with one or both parents?

_____

_____

_____

_____

_____

_____

_____

5. If we have stepsiblings, should we all pursue this dialogue together? Or are there good reasons to pursue it separately?

_____

_____

_____

_____

_____

_____

_____

6. If our parents are divorced, how would it be best to have the conversation with them: Together? Separately? With their new spouse or not?

_____

_____

_____

_____

_____

_____

_____

_____

7. Is my relationship with my parents strained in any way? What about that between my parents and my sibling(s)? If so, how might that affect our dialogue?

_____

_____

_____

_____

_____

_____

8. Are there issues we need to resolve among ourselves before we can move forward as a family? If so, what are they?

_____

_____

_____

_____

_____

_____

_____

_____

9. If it were needed, who could I/we count on for support during this dialogue? Other relatives? Spouses? Close friends? Doctor? Clergy?

_____

_____

_____

_____

_____

_____

10. If our family includes stepparents, step- or half-siblings, what is the proper means for including them (or not) in this conversation?

_____

_____

_____

_____

_____

_____

_____

_____

11. Are there any housing and/or financial issues we should discuss among ourselves before approaching our parents? For example, are any of us prepared to have Mom and/or Dad come live with us? If so, would we all be expected to contribute financially or otherwise to their care?

_____

_____

_____

_____

_____

_____

_____

12. If one or both of our parents needed and/or desired managed care and were unable to afford it, could we pay for it?

_____

_____

_____

_____

_____

_____

_____

_____

13. If our parents are in good enough health and are willing to do so, are there emotional or spiritual topics we would like to discuss with them? (For instance, emotional upsets we can resolve, unspoken feelings that would be appropriate and useful to express, questions about values and beliefs that could help us support them—or each other?)

_____

_____

_____

_____

_____

_____

_____

14. What if our parents are depressed, angry, or in denial about their growing neediness as they age—and these feelings prevent (or have prevented) them from properly planning for their old age and declining health? How can we encourage them to

participate in this dialogue anyway? Are there others we can call upon for support (trusted friends, other relatives, and so forth)? Are there certain questions we should isolate as most important and try to discuss those only? Is there some kindness or respect we can show them that would make it easier for them to participate?

_____

_____

_____

_____

_____

_____

_____

15. If either or both of them are unwilling—or unable—to talk to us, is there a trusted friend, advisor, or lawyer who could help us gather the information we believe it is necessary for us to have?

_____

_____

_____

_____

_____

_____

_____

16. Has considering all of the above caused us to think about conversations we might want to have with our own children at this time?

_____

_____

_____

_____

_____

_____

_____

_____

## ◆ CHAPTER 2 ◆

# For Parents Only

I n talking with my own (and others') parents about answering The Hard Questions with their children, I was really trying to learn about the concerns that are unique to you, the parents. The most important thing I learned from speaking with other people's parents is that many of you are also looking for ways to approach these subjects with your children. And, like us, you really don't know quite how to do that.

Like us, you're afraid of hurting or insulting your family. Like us, you tend to keep waiting for the perfect, most opportune moment, which never seems to arise. Unlike us, however, you're likely to have given more thought to these questions on your own. You're more likely than we to have considered—and backed away from, become depressed by, and/or made some peace with—your own mortality. So, although we children may think it's up to us to initiate this conversation, it is just as—or perhaps more—likely to be you who takes the first step.

Before beginning a conversation with your children about The

Hard Questions, I believe it would be helpful for you (and, if applicable, your spouse) to go over them yourselves. Identify those you can both agree to discuss and those (if any) you would prefer not to discuss. If either of you has children from another marriage, this might also be a good time to discuss how you would answer the questions with them. Figure out if one or both of you will participate in the dialogue.

If some or all of your children do *not* want to have this conversation with you, think about picking the questions whose answers are most important to you and putting those answers in writing. Then you can either give them a copy of what you have written or let them know where they are located, should the need for these answers arise. You might, for example, seal them in an envelope and give it to someone you trust—another relative, a good friend, or your lawyer or accountant—along with instructions about who should receive it if you are no longer able to care or speak for yourself. Making a written record of your thoughts and your preferences about these important subjects can also be a solution if one parent wants to have the dialogue and the other doesn't. At least the one who wants to communicate will know that he or she has made his or her wishes and thoughts known.

Before writing this, I had some very touching conversations with my own parents. I asked them how they would advise others, what they've noticed their friends doing that seemed particularly helpful—or not. Here is a sampling of their observations and advice:

- First of all, we have to remember that we are talking about adult children who, no doubt, want to be treated as adults. They can probably handle more than we think they can.
- If they don't want to have this conversation with us, we need to try to help them overcome their fear and denial of these issues.
- Most children cannot bear the thought of losing their parents. Death is a reality of life and the more our children know about our thoughts and wishes, not to mention our "estate" (such as it is), the less traumatic our aging and death will be for them.
- Don't be afraid to make the first move. While there may be reluctance on our children's part to begin with, the fact that we have initiated the conversation will at least let them know we are willing to discuss these topics. Your children may be grateful that you have made the first move.
- If your spouse doesn't want to have this discussion, go for it on your own. If some children don't want to participate, talk with those who do.
- This need not be a dismal conversation—it is informative and will provide some comfort when a parent is deceased.

- If your children approach you with The Hard Questions, it's probably best not to rush into the conversation. Tell them you'd prefer to review the questions first on your own so you can be prepared both emotionally and pragmatically.
- If you are accustomed to easy and open dialogue with your adult children, you can expect it to extend to these topics. If the ability to communicate is poor or erratic, it might be best to provide your answers in written form while also letting your children know that you will be available to discuss any or all of what you've written whenever they are ready.

No matter who initiates the conversation, however, you, the parents, are the ones with the answers. These questions are about *your* life, *your* belongings, *your* beliefs, *your* wishes. It can be very complicated to decide which questions to answer and which to leave aside. But remember, it's your prerogative to address the subjects you feel bear discussion and exclude those you don't.

17. Are we both willing to have this conversation with our children at this point in our lives? If not, can one of us move forward without the other?

_____

_____

_____

_____

_____

_____

_____

_____

18. Do we imagine our children willing to enter into this dialogue with us, or will we need to encourage them to participate?

_____

_____

_____

_____

_____

_____

19. Should all of our children participate in the conversation, or do we prefer discussing these issues with one (or some) and not others?

_____

_____

_____

_____

_____

_____

_____

_____

20. Are we both willing to divulge the financial and legal details of our lives to our children? Are there any specifics we would prefer to keep private?

_____

_____

_____

_____

_____

_____

_____

21. Are we clear between ourselves about how our possessions and other assets are to be distributed? Is any additional conversation necessary between the two of us before we discuss these issues with our children? What are we willing or unwilling to divulge about our intended bequests?

_____

_____

_____

_____

_____

_____

_____

_____

22. What information can we give our children now that will help
to make the practical issues they'll have to deal with easier after
we're gone? If we have one, do they know where our will is
kept? If we have them, do they know where our cemetery plots
are? Do they know where we keep the deed to the house and
other important papers?

_____

_____

_____

_____

_____

_____

_____

23. Do we have living wills? If so, do we each know the contents of
the other's living will? If not, are we each aware of the other's
wishes? Are we willing to share our wishes with our children?

_____

_____

_____

_____

_____

_____

_____

24. If we don't have living wills, is one or both of us interested in creating one and, if so, do we know how to do so? If not, to whom could we turn for advice? Should we ask our children to help us?

_____

_____

_____

_____

_____

_____

25. Have we made plans and/or set aside money for our long-term housing and health care needs? If so, are we willing to discuss the details with our children? If not, should we do some planning or research before we sit down to this conversation together?

_____

_____

_____

_____

_____

_____

_____

_____

26. How does each of us feel about the survivor's remarrying? Have we made financial arrangements with regard to such an eventuality? If so, should we share those arrangements with our children?

_____

_____

_____

_____

_____

_____

_____

27. If either or both of us have children from previous relationships, should these issues be discussed with all at one time, or should each of us speak with our own children separately?

_____

_____

_____

_____

_____

_____

_____

_____

28. How might each of our children relate to our death and dying, and how can we specifically support each one?

_____

_____

_____

_____

_____

_____

29. Are there things one or both of us would regret not having discussed with our children should we become unable to do so? Are there unresolved emotional issues we may wish to try to resolve? Do our children understand our spiritual beliefs and

values sufficiently to make good decisions about how we'll want to be treated as we age and remembered after we're gone?

_____

_____

_____

_____

_____

_____

_____

## ◆ CHAPTER 3 ◆

# *Family Relationships and Personal History*

For those of us who are at an age to address the issue of our parents' aging, there are likely to be big differences among the
ways we, our parents, and our own children conceive of "family history." Each generation is sure to have its own unique perspective on
stories about heritage.

For our parents, the question of where they "came from" might
be so obvious that it was never a question at all. (They might, for
example, actually still live in the town where they grew up.) Or, as
is the case for many first-generation Americans whose parents pre-
ferred to assimilate as quickly as possible, their background might
be a bit less clear to us.

Our children, on the other hand, may be members of a much
larger, more diverse family group, comprised, perhaps, of stepparents,
stepsiblings, and *their* relatives. But for each generation, knowing our
parents' (or grandparents') particular family history can be interesting,

instructive, and even healing. It can provide insight into their personalities, our own upbringing, and, for children who are being raised in a world of shifting family units, a way to feel grounded.

If you and your parents are interested, it can be wonderful to—in a sense—take their emotional and cultural history. Whenever I've had such conversations with my own parents (about the houses where they grew up, how they celebrated birthdays, what their parents were like, and so on), I've felt that I'd been offered a glimpse of a rich and complete world just before it fades into the mist. These conversations have given me a deeper understanding of who my parents are and the values they attempted to instill in me and my siblings. As a result, I feel closer to them and my self-understanding has increased as well. I, along with my brother and sister, believe that we have acquired something of value and importance to pass on to our own children.

For some families, simply sitting down and reviewing The Hard Questions about family history may be enough to spark meaningful conversation. For others, it may be more evocative to actually visit places from the past (homes, schools, churches) and simply listen to the stories that arise. They may be painful, they may be pleasant, they may simply be informative. If you think it would be valuable, you might also consider taking your own children along.

If such visits aren't practical—because the places are too far away, because your parents are no longer able to travel, or just because there isn't time—you might try to conjure up memories by sitting down with them as "armchair time-travelers." Look at family photographs together and ask your parents to tell you about the subject of each photo, the place where it was taken, and whatever stories or memories it calls to mind. You may even want to record this conversation for safekeeping.

A special note regarding painful past events: for those of us who are first- or second-generation Americans, it may be that our parents (or their parents) came to this country under difficult, painful circumstances. Perhaps they are Holocaust survivors. Perhaps they were forced to flee their country of origin. Perhaps they arrived in this country in an effort to escape poverty, dictatorship, or crime. If any one of these scenarios is true for your family, it may be too painful for your parents to discuss details of their personal history. And this may also be true for parents who suffered any other form of emotional or physical abuse. So, please, use your kindest, gentlest judgment regarding the pursuit of The Hard Questions about Family Relationships and History.

The Hard Questions about relationships are meant to help you and your parents visit issues you think are important, unresolved, or in some other way meaningful to your relationship, past and present. Some of the friends I've asked to review the questions in this book have told me that they wouldn't touch the ones about relationships with the proverbial ten-foot pole. Others, however, have said that they feel these are by far the most important questions in the book. I can certainly understand and appreciate both of these responses. These questions are meant to touch on areas that may cause each of us to feel pleased or disappointed about the other, and to share memories that make us happy or sad. It is almost guaranteed that, in varying degrees, we have all experienced these feelings. Are you interested in exploring and sharing yours? Hearing the feelings of your parents? If so, please ask these questions. If you're not sure, you might decide to choose just one question to explore and see how that goes. You might never ask another, and that would certainly be okay, but you might also find you've opened a door that allows you to explore areas you'd never visited together before.

Asking these particular questions is one time when, if you do have siblings, each one of you might prefer some "private time" with your parents. Or one of you might be open to exploring them even though others are not. And, of course, depending upon your individual family's dynamic, you might more easily discuss them as a group.

Finally, you may want to consider either asking these questions first (they can be wonderful icebreakers and lead you into discussion of more practical issues such as health care and finance) or saving them for last (once you've worked through the more practical questions). How and whenever you choose to address them, I hope these Hard Questions in particular bring you and your parents closer to one another.

30. Is there anything specific—stories, legacy, achievements, ancestry—about our family lineage that you particularly want me/us to know and remember?

_____

_____

_____

_____

_____

_____

_____

31. Do you have any photos of yourselves as children? Can we look at and label them together? Do you still have your wedding album? Can we look at and label the photos together? Can we look through and label the pictures of my/our childhood(s)?

_____

_____

_____

_____

_____

_____

_____

_____

32. What do you recall being the most enjoyable times of your life?
The most difficult?

_____

_____

_____

_____

_____

_____

_____

33. What do you hope I/we most appreciate about you?

_____

_____

_____

_____

_____

_____

_____

34. What do you most appreciate about me/us?

_____

_____

_____

_____

_____

_____

_____

35. What are/were your aspirations for me/us?

_____

_____

_____

_____

_____

_____

_____

36. What do you most want me/us to remember about our relationship?

_____

_____

_____

37. What advice would you like to give me/us about my/our life?

38. Do you have any worries about our sibling relationships when one or both of you dies?

_____

_____

39. What would you most like your grandchildren to know and remember about you?

_____

_____

_____

_____

_____

_____

_____

_____

# CHAPTER 4

# *Finances*

When it comes to discussing the difficult issues surrounding aging and death with our parents, money may be the most difficult issue of all to bring into the open. We exert our power, control, and autonomy through earning, spending, and administering our finances. No matter our age, we don't think of ourselves as self-sufficient until our income is fully self-generated. In our society, independence is generally defined as financially based, and this cultural bias can make discussing finances—particularly with our parents—especially difficult.

In addition to our fear of seeming intrusive or appearing to deny our parents their independence, many of us are raised to believe that discussing money is ill-mannered, uncouth, or inappropriate. Despite the fact that the circumstances in which we live, our plans for the future, and some of our deepest feelings of security (or insecurity) are attached to our finances, we may have been taught that raising the subject under any circumstances is taboo.

And if our parents raised us to believe that discussing money is impolite, they, no doubt, hold the same belief. But even if that isn't the case, they may not want to think about what it means to even consider relinquishing control over their financial decision-making. They may not have saved as much as they believe they should have and, therefore, they may be ashamed to discuss their economic situation. Or, they simply may not believe their children would be as capable of overseeing the details of financial management as they are. In some cases, it's also possible that our parents have made decisions about their finances that they know or believe will be hurtful to us or our siblings. For any or all of the above reasons, it can be extremely difficult for them to talk openly about money with us.

Each family's unique dynamics will come into play here. If you *can* talk openly with your parents, even this potentially painful topic may not be too difficult for you to discuss while they're still alive. But if, on the other hand, you've not been able to have difficult conversations with them in the past, it might be useful to process your feelings of sadness, shame, or anger with a friend, a spouse, a therapist, or a pastoral counselor before approaching your parents directly. Having done that, you may be better able to decide how and when to approach your parents about these particular Hard Questions—or you may decide that it's simply not possible to discuss finances at this time.

Whether or not you've been able to talk about other difficult or touchy subjects, however, you may still dread finding out about some financial disappointment or difficulty that will inevitably fall to you to resolve. Or you may simply want to delay, delay, delay because of the anxiety any discussion of money is sure to provoke. As with all hard questions, it is, nevertheless, important (and loving) *not* to procrastinate because of your own uneasiness. I'm not saying that this uneasiness isn't completely understandable—because it is! But being able to feel it and put it aside is an important step in the process of asking and answering all manner of hard questions.

Remember, making and implementing decisions about finances will require your parents' willingness and cooperation. If you are ready to move forward together, wonderful. If they are reluctant or even if they refuse, you might consider forgoing a general conversation and instead come to them with a list of options that they can choose from, or even specific papers you can leave with them to look over and, perhaps, discuss later.

And finally, if you think it will be impossible (or unnecessary) to go through all the hard questions in this chapter, by all means feel free to pick just the ones you think are most important.

40. Do you have cemetery plots? Where are they? Where is the paperwork? Are they paid in full and what's the perpetuity agreement (that is, what if any arrangements have been made to care for the plots over time)?

_____

_____

_____

_____

_____

_____

_____

_____

41. Is there any unfinished (or intended) financial business such as property sales, banking issues, or credit issues that I/we should know about?

_____

_____

_____

_____

_____

_____

42. How many bank accounts do you have and in which banks are they located? Who are the signatories on each account? How might I/we access these accounts, should you become incapacitated? If you bank online, what passwords are required to access the accounts?

_____

_____

_____

_____

_____

_____

_____

_____

43. If I/we need them, where could I/we locate your last seven years of tax returns?

_____

_____

_____

_____

_____

_____

_____

44. If relevant, who is your stockbroker, who is your financial planner, and what is their contact information?

_____

_____

_____

_____

_____

_____

_____

_____

45. Do you have an accountant, and, if so, can you give me/us his/her contact information?

_____

_____

_____

_____

_____

_____

_____

46. If you have unfinished financial business you feel unable to complete, is there any way I/we can help?

_____

_____

_____

_____

_____

_____

_____

_____

47. Are all of your assets owned jointly or are some in the name of one of you only? If the latter, what happens to those assets if the one who "owns" them is the first to die?

_____

_____

_____

_____

_____

_____

_____

_____

48. If either or both of you have children from other relationships, do you have any concerns or have you made any decisions regarding those children that we should discuss?

_____

_____

_____

_____

_____

_____

_____

49. Have you considered that one of you might remarry? If so, have you made any provision to deal with inheritance issues that might arise?

_____

_____

_____

_____

_____

_____

50. Do you have money set aside and specifically designated for long-term health care or assisted living should either or both of you become unable to live alone? Do you know what services are covered by your medical insurance?

_____

_____

_____

_____

_____

_____

_____

51. Who would you like to make financial decisions for you should you become incapable of making them yourself?

_____

_____

_____

_____

_____

_____

_____

52. Have you considered putting your money into a trust to help me/us protect and preserve your savings?

_____

_____

_____

_____

_____

_____

_____

53. If appropriate, can we see a lawyer together so that he or she can explain to you what your options are for protecting your assets?

_____

_____

_____

_____

_____

_____

_____

54. If you're uncomfortable talking about the details of your financial situation with me/us, is there someone else (your lawyer, accountant, or insurance agent) you could authorize me/us to speak with?

_____

_____

_____

_____

_____

_____

_____

# ✦ CHAPTER 5 ✦

# Possessions, Legalities, and Paperwork

When my parents reached their late sixties, they started joking with us about who would get what after they had passed. If I complimented my mother on a necklace she was wearing, she would say "so . . . does that mean you want it after I'm gone?" If my father saw me looking at a painting in their house, he would tease, "I'll put you down for that in my will if you can get ready for dinner in the next ten minutes." (If you, too, come from a family that uses humor to defuse—and sometimes obfuscate—delicate psychological issues, you will understand the spirit of this joking.)

Over the next several years, however, the jocular nature of these exchanges gradually became more serious. As we sat together in my parents' living room, they would begin trying to introduce the subject of "who wants what." My response and that of my siblings was always along the lines of, "Can we please not talk about this right now?" Luckily, my parents are brave, practical, and persistent. If they couldn't get a consensus from the group, they would seek individual answers. And so they began inserting this topic into the course of our everyday conversations. It was always handled very simply. One or the other would say, "Is there anything in our house you feel particularly attached to? We're talking all this over with our lawyer, and it would really help us to know." Their informal tone—combined with the fact that they had no pressing health issues at the time—allowed each of us the freedom to honestly indicate our particular sentimental attachments.

Whether or not you come from a family of means, the circumstances under which you were raised are always rich—rich with hope and fear, gain and loss, happiness and sorrow. And this richness of meaning is often contained, reflected, or triggered by physical objects. It's also true, of course, that "stuff" has commercial value. What's important here is not to confuse the two. For both parents and children, it's important *not* to try to right past wrongs through the exchange of material possessions.

*Children:* If there are psychological or spiritual issues that need attention, don't expect them to be worked out in your parents' last will and testament. Try to work through these issues in another forum.

*Parents:* Remember that these are your belongings, and you have the right to do with them exactly as you wish—but try not to send messages about your feelings through the way you construct your will. Or at least be as clear as possible (either in conversation or in writing) about why you're doing what you're doing so that your children will have some way of understanding your intent. Of course, it would be most helpful to simply discuss these issues together with your children. Use the questions in this chapter to begin that dialogue, and feel free to make up any that you think might be more relevant to your particular situation.

No matter what is discussed and/or decided regarding possessions, one of two things will be true: Your parents either do or do not have paperwork documenting these decisions or any other thoughts and wishes. Needless to say, it's always helpful to know what files or papers, if any, they have and where they're kept. If there are no such papers, that's also useful to know.

55. Would you like to speak with me/us now about your belongings and how you would like them to be divided, even though this may be specified in your will?

---

---

---

_____

_____

_____

_____

_____

56. Which of your belongings would you like me/us to keep? Are there any special family heirlooms I/we should know about? If so, what are they and whom would you like to have them?

_____

_____

_____

_____

_____

_____

_____

57. What arrangements would you like me/us to make for your pet(s) if you are no longer able to take care of them and/or after your death?

_____

_____

_____

_____

_____

_____

_____

_____

58. After you're gone, are there any relationships, clubs, organizations, charities, or activities that you'd like me/us to stay connected to in any way, on your behalf?

_____

_____

_____

_____

_____

_____

59. Is there a particular charity or other organization to which you would like me/us to donate some of your belongings?

_____

_____

_____

_____

_____

60. Is there anyone else—either a family member or a friend—to whom you would like to give a particular memento of your life?

_____

_____

_____

_____

_____

_____

_____

61. Would you like your home to remain in the family, or do you have any other preferences concerning the ownership or occupation of the family home?

_____

_____

_____

_____

_____

_____

_____

62. Where are your household repair/purchase records? Where are the deed and title to your house? Other property?

_____

_____

_____

_____

_____

_____

_____

63. Do you feel comfortable telling me/us what (if any) arrangements you have made for your real property?

_____

_____

_____

_____

_____

_____

_____

64. Are there any possessions or property I/we might not know about or be able to locate that you would like to tell me/us about now?

_____

_____

_____

_____

_____

_____

_____

_____

65. Is there any unfinished legal business (such as real estate transactions, complaints, or lawsuits) that I/we should know about? If there is a lawyer involved, what is his or her contact information?

_____

_____

_____

_____

_____

_____

66. Do either or both of you have life insurance? If so, is there anything about the policy or the way you would like the money to be used that I/we ought to know now? Who is/are the benefici-

ary(ies)? Is your policy referenced in your will? Has the face amount been reduced by loans against the policy?

_____

_____

_____

_____

_____

_____

_____

67. Do you have a safety deposit box? If so, who besides yourself has keys, where are they kept, and what is the location of the box(es)? Is the person holding the second key aware of the procedures for and means of access?

_____

_____

_____

_____

_____

_____

_____

68. Where are your birth certificates kept?

_____

_____

_____

_____

_____

_____

_____

69. Do you have any assets in custodial care, that is, in someone's name (such as a broker, lawyer, or other relative) for safekeeping that you may or may not want to remain with that person after your death?

_____

_____

_____

_____

_____

_____

_____

70. Do you have a will? Where is it kept? Who is the attorney of record?

_____

_____

_____

_____

_____

_____

_____

_____

_____

71. Who is/are the executor(s) of your will? Is/are the executor(s) aware of his or her role?

_____

_____

_____

_____

_____

_____

_____

72. Have you given anyone your power of attorney? If so, who? Is it for general or specific purposes?

_____

_____

_____

_____

_____

_____

_____

_____

73. Have you considered writing a "Letter of Instruction," laying out your wishes about organ donation, funeral and burial arrangements, specifics about personal wishes, or other issues not typically addressed in a will?

_____

_____

_____

_____

_____

_____

_____

74. Who would you like to make legal decisions for you, should you become incapable of making them yourself? Is this person aware of your wishes?

_____

_____

_____

_____

_____

_____

_____

_____

75. If you're uncomfortable talking about your legal situation(s) with me/us, is there someone else (your lawyer or accountant) with whom you might authorize me/us to speak?

_____

_____

_____

_____

_____

_____

_____

_____

## ♦ CHAPTER 6 ♦

# Health Care and Quality
# of Life

Sadly, several of my friends have found themselves in the unfortunate but not unusual, terrifying, and disturbing position of having to make very, very important health-related decisions for their parents. One friend (whose mother has Alzheimer's disease) kept bringing up the subject of managed care with her, hoping for a mutual decision, until he realized that his mother was no longer capable of co-authoring this decision: Her cognitive abilities were simply too impaired. At that point it became clear that any decision-making would fall to him alone.

Another friend found herself stepping in and assuming day-to-day decision-making responsibility for her ferociously self-sufficient father, who was recovering from heart surgery and had, in addition, fallen into a deep depression when his wife had a serious accident that required surgery of her own. Both her father's depression and her mother's injuries required important, on-the-spot decisions about health care, finances, and legalities. As a result, my friend found herself in charge of myriad important family details.

A third friend found herself in the situation every adult child probably dreads most—having to decide whether or not to keep her father on life support.

In each of these situations, my friends expressed a similar wish: that they could be reasonably confident that the choices they were making were those *their parents would have made for themselves*. Of course, there is no way of being absolutely certain—and no healthy parent's answer to the hard questions about health care should be assumed to apply unequivocally if that parent becomes ill. And yet, all of these adult children were trying their best to do what their parents would have wanted.

Short of a full-blown health care crisis, it is possible that, as the years pass, some diminution of physical and/or mental capability will occur—anything from forgetting where the car keys are to forgetting how to drive. At some point, parents may begin to wonder whether they can continue to manage certain everyday tasks, or, more likely, children may begin to realize that some type of intervention is necessary. This realization is clearly an epic turning point—albeit one that is as likely to creep up slowly ("Mom seems to be having trouble going up and down the stairs") as it is to hit us in the face ("Dad has had a small stroke"). When that happens, it's completely natural to hope things will "go back to normal" as quickly as possible. We want this very, very badly for our emotional comfort. Sometimes it's possible. Sometimes it's not. If it's not, we must accept the reality that the time has come to begin shifting (or sharing) the responsibility for maintaining our parents' quality of life.

There is simply no way to make these kinds of decisions easily. One thing that can make it a bit less difficult, however, is for each to know the other's wishes, worst fears, and emotional, financial, and spiritual capabilities and limitations. The Hard Questions can help to at least generate such a list.

Should your parents become chronically ill, are there habits of daily life you all might be too embarrassed to talk about that could really contribute to their continued sense of dignity and courage in the face of illness? These might include personal care ("It's important to me that I continue getting my hair done"); habitual activities such as going to church, playing cards, a regular movie date with friends, or attending events connected with professional associations; or maintaining the support of causes that are important to one or both of them. Their ability to continue these activities—as well as their knowledge that you understand and are willing to support their wishes and intentions as to how time and resources should be spent—can be crucial to their ongoing mental and emotional well-being. The more you know about your parents' particular wishes with regard to the character and quality of their everyday life, the easier it will be for you to support their essential humanity.

This—the wish to both preserve and support essential human dignity—is also at the heart of The Hard Questions regarding housing arrangements, should one or both parents become incapable of living (or no longer desire to live) independently. The answers to these questions can have significant emotional and financial consequences. And, as with other Hard Questions, it can be very tricky to keep the emotional separate from the financial. The more you can discuss the subject openly before any such need arises, the better both you and your parents will be able to make good decisions if and when the time does come. For instance, I was surprised to hear my mother and father say that, no matter what, they didn't want to live with any of their children. They had two reasons—they didn't want to "be a burden" to any of us *and* they imagined they would prefer being with people their own age. We would never have guessed this, although it makes perfect sense. Other families may feel exactly the opposite. And, of course, once your parents' preferences are known, it's important to determine whether it will be possible, financially and otherwise, to support their wishes—and if not, to discuss alternate plans until you are able to arrive at a solution that makes sense both emotionally and financially.

Because it's almost impossible to approach these questions matter-of-factly, without calling up your own and your parents' worst fears, it's vital that the conversation proceed thoughtfully and gently. If possible, leave plenty of time for this dialogue to unfold. Be sensitive to your own and your parents' tolerance for the subject, and don't press too hard.

That said, however, as with all the Hard Questions—but particularly these—it would be useful to begin the discussion as early as possible, when there's still time to begin investigating and take advantage of financial options, such as Medicare, Medicaid, and long-term health insurance. In addition to which, you will probably want to find out (while it is still possible to do so and before it becomes an emergency) whether your parents have a living will or have otherwise made known their wishes about prolonging life in various circumstances.

In the end, asking and answering these questions can provide reassurance to parents that their wishes are known and to children that they are carrying out those wishes to the best of their ability.

76. Who are your doctors? In addition to your family physician, do you see any specialists? What is their contact information? Are

you currently undergoing (or planning to undergo) a course of treatment for a particular condition?

_____

_____

_____

_____

_____

_____

_____

_____

77. What hospital would you prefer to be taken to, should the need arise?

_____

_____

_____

_____

_____

_____

_____

78. Do you have health insurance? Medicare? Medicaid? Medicare Supplemental Insurance? Does it cover all your medical needs

and expenses? Would you like me/us to review your health insurance policies with you?

_____

_____

_____

_____

_____

_____

_____

79. Have you been diagnosed with any chronic illnesses—for example, diabetes, high blood pressure, arthritis, emphysema, or heart disease? Have you been diagnosed with any psychiatric disorders, such as depression or anxiety disorder?

_____

_____

_____

_____

_____

_____

_____

_____

80. Are you taking any medications? What for? How often? Where do you prefer to purchase them? Is their cost covered by insurance?

_____

_____

_____

_____

_____

_____

_____

81. Let's discuss your driving. Do you still feel comfortable behind the wheel? Do others feel comfortable with you behind the wheel? Do I/we? Can I/we establish some way of discussing your driving should it deteriorate and you are unable or unwilling to admit it?

_____

_____

_____

_____

_____

_____

_____

_____

82. Are there any everyday tasks or chores you'd like me/us to look
after should you become too infirm to do so on your own, even
if you feel uncomfortable asking (for instance, take you to the
doctor, the dentist, or the hairdresser, maintain magazine sub-
scriptions, continue weekly lunches or other meetings)?

_____

_____

_____

_____

_____

_____

_____

83. Would you like me/us to have a key to your home in case of a
medical emergency? Is there anyone else—a neighbor or em-
ployee, for example—who has one?

_____

_____

_____

_____

_____

_____

_____

_____

84. If you can't take care of yourself physically, where would you prefer to live? At home, with care? In an assisted living facility? What if one of you becomes incapacitated and the other isn't? Have you made any arrangements for such an eventuality? If so, what are they? If not, what can I/we do to support and carry out your wishes?

_____

_____

_____

_____

_____

_____

_____

85. If you become ill or depressed, are there others—family, friends, clergy—whom you would like me to ask to visit you? Pray for you?

_____

_____

_____

_____

_____

_____

_____

_____

86. Whom would you like to make health care decisions for you if you are not capable of making them yourself? Have you created a Health Care Proxy or designated a Health Care Agent? If so, where is it kept/who is it? If not, would you like me/us to help you make this decision?

_____

_____

_____

_____

_____

_____

87. Have you made a living will? If so, would you like to share the contents with me/us? If not, would you like to discuss your preferences or thoughts about living with pain, limiting (or not) life-support treatment under various circumstances such as

irreversible coma, permanent brain damage, or any other situation you can imagine? If you would like to create a living will but don't know how, would you like me/us to help you figure it out?

_____

_____

_____

_____

_____

_____

_____

88. If you should be diagnosed with a terminal illness, under what circumstances (if any) would you want a "Do Not Resuscitate" order followed? If you don't know how to answer this question, would you like me/us to help you research possible answers?

_____

_____

_____

_____

_____

_____

_____

89. As much as you can imagine now, do you have a preference for where you would like to die—in a hospital, hospice, or at home?

_____

_____

_____

_____

_____

_____

_____

90. Do you wish to donate organs? If so, is this wish documented anywhere, such as on your driver's license or in your living will? In any case, would you like to make your wishes known to me/us?

_____

_____

_____

_____

_____

_____

_____

## ◆ CHAPTER 7 ◆

# *Spirituality*

This chapter contains the fewest questions, but answering them together can yield the information most likely to support your parents through the difficulties of aging and you through the grieving process. What are your parents' beliefs about what happens upon death? How do they wish to be remembered? What happens to the feelings you have for one another after they're gone? Contemplating these questions together can help parents connect (or reconnect) to the beliefs that might alleviate some of the fear that goes along with their aging. And it can help children understand how best to care for and remember their parents—in the ways *they* would like to be cared for and remembered. This knowing in itself can be of enormous comfort.

Each family will need to decide whether or not asking and answering these questions is appropriate for them—although my guess is that all or some of them will be meaningful for people of any background. Whether we come from a family that is strongly religious (and, therefore, consider the answers to be self-evident), or from a family of atheists, most of us have individual notions about death, spirit, and what—if anything—comes after death. If your family is deeply and traditionally religious, your parents may, nevertheless, have a uniquely personal way of viewing or interpreting the teachings of their religion. And if they do not practice their religion of birth, or subscribe to no religious tradition at all, they might still have their own very personal spiritual beliefs.

If it is appropriate and possible, I would urge you to learn about your parents' spiritual beliefs, wishes, hopes, and fears. No matter what the answers turn out to be, they will help you to offer them whatever it is they need as they contend with the realities of aging and death.

There is nothing I, or anyone, can say to eradicate all the pain of these realities. But there is one thing that can *always* help—before, during, and after suffering a loss—and that is love. Love born of courage and tenderheartedness, love of self and other in perfect balance, love that opens and receives and is not afraid to be with what is, as it arises.

91. Should you become seriously or terminally ill, are there any actions or rituals you would like to be carried out on your behalf: certain prayers or contemplative practices, music you would like to hear, people you would like to have by your side or oth-

erwise hear from, items you would like placed near you such as flowers, photographs, books, or religious or spiritual images?

_____

_____

_____

_____

_____

_____

_____

92. What are your funeral wishes? Have you made arrangements for those wishes to be met? If so, what are they? If not, would you like to tell me/us your wishes and ask for my/our help?

_____

_____

_____

_____

_____

_____

_____

93. Whom would you like to preside over your burial, memorial service, and/or memorial event?

_____

_____

_____

_____

_____

_____

_____

_____

94. Are there any specific words, poems, and/or Bible readings
    you'd like read at your funeral? What, if anything, would you
    like said or done at your funeral?

_____

_____

_____

_____

_____

_____

95. Would you like to specify what is to be said on your grave-
    stone? If cremated, would you like to specify what is to be done
    with your ashes?

_____

_____

_____

_____

_____

_____

_____

96. What traditions would you like me/us to continue as a family, and/or in my/our own families?

_____

_____

_____

_____

_____

_____

97. What can I/we do, think, say, or be to carry the meaning of your life with me/us?

_____

_____

_____

_____

_____

_____

_____

_____

98. When I/we need your love after you're gone, what can I/we do, think, say, or remember to evoke our heart connection?

_____

_____

_____

_____

_____

_____

99. What, if any, are your beliefs about what happens when you die? Do you believe in an afterlife, reincarnation, after-death communication, and/or something else?

_____

_____

_____

_____

_____

_____

_____

_____

100. Are there any religious, spiritual, and/or other rutials you would like me/us to observe to remember you and mark the anniversary of your death?

_____

_____

_____

_____

_____

_____

_____

_____

# AFTERWORD

Both writing this book and answering these questions with my own parents have been extraordinary experiences. It's been scary for all of us, not to mention at times sad and uncomfortable. As we've moved through these questions, there have been many tears and also, believe it or not, a lot of humor and laughing. But, at the heart of the experience there has been a continual sense of deepening love. As we've opened ourselves to this dialogue, to our feelings, fears, and memories both painful and pleasant, we've opened our hearts to one another in a very simple and direct way. I wish you and your family the ability to stand together in a similarly loving space.

For more information on this process, please visit *www.thehardquestions.com*.

# GLOSSARY AND CHECKLISTS

*Advance Directives*

Advance Directives are written documents a competent individual creates to specify his or her wishes regarding health care matters, should he or she become incapable (as determined by a physician) of making decisions. Depending on your state's laws, they may or may not be legally binding. Typically, Advance Directives include:

- Anatomical Gifts/Organ Donation

- Code/No Code or Do Not Resuscitate (DNR)

- Durable Power of Attorney for Health Care

- Living Will

Different states have different laws for honoring Advance Directives—so be sure to investigate your state's laws regarding such documents.

Note that in the absence of such directives, you will have no control over decisions regarding health care and quality of life if you are incapacitated.

Visit this link: *http://www.uslegalforms.com/poweratty.htm* to find the proper legal documents for your state.

*Anatomical Gifts/Organ Donation*

You may choose to donate all or part of your body for medical research. If you choose to do so, depending on your state's laws and regulations, you may specify your intentions on your Driver's License, in a Living Will, or simply in a notarized document. Often, hospitals have a procedure for verifying a patient's wishes. All fifty states have a version of the Uniform Anatomical Gift Act, which allows a person to make a gift of organs and tissues upon death. If you have made no wishes known in advance, family members may make such decisions for you. So if you have strong preferences, it's good to make them known.

Some questions to consider:

- Do I wish to donate any organs or tissue?

- If so, do I have a preference about where and for what purpose they be donated?

- Am I prepared to, and do I know how to, document my preferences in a way that is legally recognized in my state?

- Do I spend time in another state and also need my wishes documented there?

## Code/No Code or Do Not Resuscitate (DNR)

"Code" and "No Code" are terms used by medical professionals. "Code" means that CPR should be used and "No Code" means that it shouldn't. "Do Not Resuscitate" also means that CPR should not be used. You may choose to forgo CPR if your body is too weak to withstand the physical pressure of this procedure and/or if you do not wish to prolong your life. Your wishes regarding "Code," "No Code," and "DNR" can be made in a Living Will, stated orally, or, if you are incapable (as determined by your doctor) of making this decision yourself, by a surrogate decision-maker.

## Durable Power of Attorney for Health Care (DPOAH-C)

This document specifies the person who is to make health care decisions on your behalf, should you become unable to. Some states require this as part of a Living Will, others allow them to be separate documents.

*Executor*

An Executor is the person or entity you name in your will to carry out the terms and provisions of that will.

Some questions to consider:

Have I decided who is to be the Executor of my will?

Does that person or entity know of his/her role?

Is there anything specific I should go over with my Executor at this time?

*Health Care Proxy or Agent*

A Health Care Proxy or Agent is someone whom you have authorized to make health care (and only health care) decisions for you should you become unable (as determined by a physician) to make such decisions yourself.

The decision to appoint a Health Care Proxy or Agent can be memorialized by what is sometimes called a Durable Power of Attorney for Health Care or DPOAH-C. (Different states have different names for this document.) Most forms enable your Proxy or Agent to make any and all health care decisions for you, even if others— say, other relatives, clergy, even your spouse—disagree. So choose this person very carefully, as his or her decision may be the final word. Your Agent must be over eighteen years old, have a thorough understanding of your wishes, and be able to take a stand on your behalf.

Some questions to consider before choosing a Health Care Agent:

Does this person really understand my wishes and beliefs about death and dying?

Do I trust this person to stand up for my wishes and beliefs should I be unable to do so?

Is this person willing and able to become my Agent?

Who might be a good alternate if my Agent is unable to carry out this responsibility for any reason?

Am I prepared to memorialize my decisions in a Living Will? If so, do I know where to find the appropriate documents? Do I understand my state's legal position on Living Wills?

Do I spend time in another state and also need my wishes documented there?

*Letter of Instruction*

A Letter of Instruction is a non–legally binding document you can prepare for your spouse or children that contains information about location of assets, procedures for collecting benefits, religious procedures to follow during death and dying, and instructions for funeral arrangements. In this document, you can specify whom you wish notified of your death, addresses and contact information for bank accounts and other financial holdings, credit card account information, and instructions for giving items of sentimental value. A Letter of Instruction can cover myriad small but important details and be a valuable guide for your loved ones.

Some things to consider including in a Letter of Instruction:

- *Banking:* Account numbers, bank locations, online access and passwords, signatories.

- *Benefits:* Veterans, Social Security, or Employment benefits due or expected.

- *Credit Cards:* Account numbers, outstanding balances, procedures for closing account(s).

- *Debts:* A list of monies owed by you or to you.

- *Gifts:* Personal items you would like to give to specific people or entities.

- *Important Papers*: Location of tax returns, mortgage, automobile registration, deeds to house or other property, artwork authentication papers, etc.

- *Insurance Policies*: Auto, Homeowners, Life, Medical, etc., and their policy numbers, agents, and contact information.

- *Religious and Spiritual Wishes*: Rites you would like performed, how you would like your body to be treated, who you would like to pray for you, what prayers you would like offered on your behalf.

- *Safety Deposit Box(es)*: Location of and procedures for access.

- *Stocks and Bonds*: Names and addresses of brokers, list of transactions.

## Living Will

A Living Will is a document in which an individual considers the possibility of becoming incapacitated and specifies preferences for various types of care under a number of circumstances. Questions to consider in creating a Living Will include "Do I want to be kept on life support if I'm in a coma with no hope of recovery?" "Do I want to continue to receive pain medication if I'm in a coma?" "Would I like to donate my organs and, if so, for medical research and/or educational purposes or only for those persons needing transplants?"

A Living Will becomes active only when and if its creator becomes incapacitated.

A Living Will can be changed or cancelled at any time.

Since one can't provide direction for any and all future possibilities, it's advisable to also appoint a Health Care Agent, someone who holds your Health Care Proxy and whom you trust to make decisions in your best interests.

Some questions to consider before making a Living Will:

- Do I want to be kept on life support if I'm in a coma with no hope of awakening?

- Do I want to be kept on life support if I'm in a persistent vegetative state?

- If I have an incurable illness, do I want to continue to receive procedures and treatments? If so, up until what point do I want efforts made to prolong my life?

- If I'm on life support, do I still want to receive pain medications?

- If I choose to forgo procedures or treatments, do I still want to receive pain medication?

- Am I prepared to memorialize my decisions in a Living Will? If so, do I know where to find the appropriate documents? Do I understand my state's legal position on Living Wills?

- Do I spend time in another state and also need my wishes documented there?

## Power of Attorney

A "POA" is a legal document wherein an individual designates another person to act on his/her behalf as long as the individual does not become disabled or incapacitated. A "durable" power of attorney is effective after you are incapacitated. You can give general Power of Attorney, giving someone the right to make any and all legal decisions on your behalf, or you can give specific Power of Attorney (for example, for health care only, or real estate only).

## Safety Deposit Box and Rules for Access

Laws vary greatly from state to state regarding accessing Safety Deposit Boxes, which can be owned individually or jointly. Generally speaking, if the safety deposit box is owned individually, the bank may require a certified copy of the death certificate and letters of administration before granting access. Call your attorney or bank for rules regarding co-owned safety deposit boxes.

Although it is always best to consult an attorney, you may visit the following to obtain legal forms:

*www.findlegalforms.com*

*www.itslegal.com*

*www.legalzoom.com*

*www.partnershipforcaring.org*

*www.uslegalforms.com*

For additional support, please visit the following:

American Association of Retired Persons: *www.aarp.com*

Aging with Dignity: *www.agingwithdignity.org*

American Bar Association's Commission on Legal Problems of the Elderly: *www.abanet.org/aging*

American Medical Directors Association: *www.amda.com/links/healthaging.htm*

# 10 IMPORTANT QUESTIONS
## TO ASK IN AN ACUTE SITUATION

If you've come to this book at a time of critical need—an ill parent has taken a turn for the worse, a well parent has suddenly taken seriously ill or even died—here is a short list of questions that can be helpful under urgent circumstances.

If it's possible to dialogue with your parent directly, try and do so during a quiet moment, should one arise. If it isn't possible, try to go over these questions together with your other parent, siblings, another relative, trusted family friend, or care provider. These are the questions you are likely to be called upon to make quick decisions about.

1. If you have a terminal illness, under what circumstances (if any) would you want a "Do Not Resuscitate" order followed? If you don't know how to answer this question, would you like me to review the options with your doctor and tell them to you?

2. As much as you can imagine now, do you have a preference for where you would like to die—in a hospital, hospice, or at home?

3. Do you wish to donate organs? If so, is this wish documented anywhere, such as on your driver's license or in your living will?

In any case, would you like to make your wishes known to me/us?

4. If you are seriously or terminally ill, are there any actions or rituals you would like to be carried out on your behalf: certain prayers or contemplative practices, music you would like to hear, people you would like to have by your side or otherwise hear from, items you would like placed near you such as flowers, photographs, books, or religious or spiritual images?

5. Do you have a will? Where is it kept? Who is the attorney of record?

6. Have you given anyone your power of attorney? If so, who? Is it for general or specific purposes?

7. Have you made a living will? If so, would you like to share the contents with me/us? If not, would you like me/us to list options and choices about living with pain, receiving nourishment, and limiting (or not) life-support treatments?

8. What are your funeral wishes? Have you made arrangements for those wishes to be met? If not, would you like to tell me/us your wishes?

9. Do you have a cemetery plot? Where is it?

10. Are there any specific words, poems, and/or Bible readings you'd like read at your funeral? What, if anything, would you like said or done at your funeral?